Anything is POSSIBLE

Inspiring true stories for tween boys about courage, dreaming big, and never giving up.

TWEEN SUCCESS

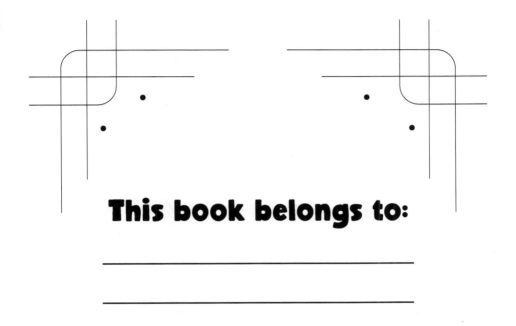

This book belongs to:

_____

_____

_____

SOMETHING
FOR YOU

Get your <u>FREE</u> Printable Workbook!

To download your free workbook

SCAN
HERE

Table of Contents

It all starts here...

I've got a secret to share with you... a secret that will change your life. This secret has the power to make all your dreams come true. It's the key to success, happiness, and a bright future.

The secret is simple:

ANYTHING IS POSSIBLE.

Yes, anything. You can be whoever you want to be, do whatever you dream of doing and achieve anything you set your mind to. Just imagine what you could do if you genuinely believed anything was possible.

IT'S ALL ABOUT HAVING THE COURAGE TO PURSUE YOUR DREAMS, THE SELF-BELIEF TO KNOW THAT YOU CAN ACHIEVE THEM, AND THE PERSEVERANCE TO KEEP GOING WHEN THINGS GET TOUGH.

This book will explore what it means to dream big and work hard and how having the right mindset is the key to a successful life. We'll meet inspiring people who have overcome failure to achieve their goals and learned that failure is part of success.

You might have already heard of some of the people we'll meet. Others, you'll learn about for the first time. But they all have one thing in common: They refused to give up on their dreams, no matter what.

Take Nelson Mandela, for example. Mandela dreamed of a day when all people would be treated equally, regardless of the color of their skin. He spent 27 years in prison fighting for his dream, and he eventually became the first democratically elected president of South Africa.

Or what about Jaylen Arnold? When he was just three years old, he was diagnosed with Tourette syndrome and bullied at school because of his condition. But Jaylen used his experiences to become an anti-bullying activist and motivational speaker. He's now helping other kids who are being bullied and showing them that anything is possible.

We'll also meet:
- An entrepreneur who was turned down for a job at KFC and is now a billionaire.

- A self-taught inventor who, at just 14 years old, built a windmill out of junk to supply electricity to his home.

- A physicist considered a slow learner who left school at 16 but is regarded as one of the most outstanding scientists of all time.

- A former wrestler who is now one of the most successful movie stars in the world.

But before we begin, there's one more thing...

THIS IS YOUR BOOK.

Yes, yours.

MAKE IT WHATEVER YOU WANT IT TO BE.

So go ahead — color outside the lines, write in the margins, and add your own stories and illustrations. This book is for you, and it's meant to be used however you see fit.

Now let's get started on this journey together. Are you ready?

ANYTHING IS POSSIBLE!

It always seems

IMPOSSIBLE

UNTIL it's

DONE.

- Nelson Mandela

CHAPTER 1

COURAGE & THE POWER OF POSITIVE THINKING

He who is NOT COURAGEOUS enough to TAKE RISKS will ACCOMPLISH NOTHING in life.

- Muhammad Ali

Sometimes it's easier to say no than to face our fears and take risks. But to achieve big dreams, you need to be brave and have the courage to take chances.

Say yes to OPPORTUNITIES, even when you're scared.
Be okay with making mistakes, and TRY AGAIN.
Learn from your failures and KEEP GOING.
BELIEVE IN YOURSELF, even if no one else does.

That's what true courage is all about.

Being courageous doesn't mean you're never afraid. Everyone feels fear at some point in their lives. Courage is about facing those fears and doing what you want to do anyway. It's about following your dreams, even when it's scary.

So how do you become more courageous? A lot of it has to do with your mindset.

If you believe that you can't do something, then you probably won't even try. But if you think anything is possible, you're more likely to take risks and achieve your goals.

That's why having a positive outlook is so important. It's not just about thinking optimistically—it's about believing in yourself and your abilities.

YOU CAN DO IT!

When you have that mindset, anything is possible. As the people in the stories below will show you, a bit of courage and a positive attitude can go a long way.

Jaylen Arnold

ANTI-BULLYING ACTIVIST (2000 – PRESENT)

Jaylen Arnold is a leading American activist in the
fight against bullying.

> **≈ I'm trying to make THE WORLD a BETTER place in any way that I CAN. ≈**
>
> **- Jaylen Arnold**

Bullies never win.

This is something that Jaylen Arnold knows all too well, having been bullied himself when he was younger. Instead of letting the bullies win, Arnold used his experiences to become an anti-bullying activist and speaker, working to make the world a better place for everyone.

Born in Florida in August 2000, Arnold has been on a mission to stop bullying since he was just a young boy.

When he was only three years old, Arnold was diagnosed with Tourette syndrome. This condition makes it difficult to control your body. People with Tourette's often make noises and move around without meaning to. These noises and movements are called "tics." Because of this, Arnold was teased mercilessly and became the target of bullies at his school.

Tourette's is not the only condition Arnold suffers from. When he was four years old, doctors confirmed that he also has obsessive-compulsive disorder (OCD), which causes unwanted thoughts to appear in your brain or gives you an almost uncontrollable urge to repeat the same action.

Then, at eight, Arnold was diagnosed with Asperger's syndrome. This condition makes it hard for people to interact socially.

These challenges must have made life extremely difficult for the young boy, but Arnold decided to turn his pain into something positive. In the same year he was diagnosed with Asperger's, at just eight years of age, he established his own non-profit charity, the Jaylen's Challenge Foundation, which educates teachers and kids about bullying and how to stop it.

Although he started with just a website, Arnold soon handed out glow-in-the-dark wristbands with his slogan "Bullying no way!" to anyone who supported his cause.

Arnold wants differently-abled kids like himself to be able to live without being mocked or bullied. Instead of fighting back against bullying with his fists, he used his words and activism.

Rather than shame bullies and make them feel small, Arnold would prefer to teach them tolerance and respect towards others and spread the message that it's ok to be different.

The Jaylen's Challenge Foundation soon gained the attention of "The Ellen Show" and CNN. Arnold has since received support from plenty of important people.

Hollywood stars like Leonardo DiCaprio have worn Arnold's bracelet, and basketball star LeBron James has partnered with him on some projects. He even met UK royals Prince William and Prince Harry when he became the only American recipient of the Princess Diana Legacy Award at age 16.

Arnold has also worked closely with Dash Mihok, a TV star who has suffered from Tourette's since the age of six and has become a spokesperson for the Jaylen's Challenge Foundation. Together, the pair raised $57,000 for the US Tourette Syndrome Association (TSA) in 2010 through the "One Lap Closer to a Cure" marathon held at Walt Disney World in Florida.

This is just one of this young activist's many impressive accomplishments. Arnold has spoken to over 240,000 young people at hundreds of schools across 31 American states about his cause. He has also been included in the Reader's Digest list of "14 Incredible Kids Who Changed the World in the Last Decade".

Arnold's incredible achievements are even more remarkable, considering that he has had to deal with challenges far more significant than the average boy.

Rather than letting the weight of these challenges stop him, Arnold has made a difference in the lives of thousands of young people through his determination.

Today, Arnold is a young adult studying film at Southeastern University in Florida, with aspirations to one day make it big as a Hollywood producer. He is also a popular and successful public speaker and has appeared as an actor in short films. He has continued to prioritize his work through his foundation and still travels around to spread his anti-bullying message whenever possible.

It is tough to go through childhood with a disorder like Tourette's syndrome. When you add OCD and Asperger's, life for Arnold must have been quite hard, even without bullying making it more complicated.

BUT INSTEAD OF LETTING THE BULLIES BRING HIM DOWN, ARNOLD CHOSE TO RISE ABOVE THEM AND BECOME AN EXAMPLE OF STRENGTH AND COURAGE FOR OTHERS.

Arnold has taught differently-abled people to love and accept themselves for who they are. While educating young people that it's not ok to bully people who are different. Arnold is making the world a better place, one day at a time.

Arnold's story is about being true to yourself and accepting who you are. It is also a reminder that we all have something unique to offer the world, no matter our circumstances. Arnold is living proof of the influential roles that courage and positive thinking can play in helping overcome any hardship.

Rick Allen

MUSICIAN (1963 – PRESENT)

Rick Allen is the drummer for the English hard rock
band, Def Leppard.

If you're

thrown in the

DEEP END,

you SWIM,

and that's basically

WHAT I DID.

I HAD TO...

— Rick Allen

You might have heard the saying, "Through adversity comes strength." This means that the more difficult experiences we have in life, the stronger we become. Rick Allen is a perfect example of this.

Born in November 1963 in the small town of Dronfield, England, Allen became the drummer for world-famous hard rockers Def Leppard, when he was just 15 years old. Today, he's recognized by music fans as one of the greatest drummers of all time.

But Allen's career almost came to a tragic and early end. On New Year's Eve, 1984, when he was 21 years old, he lost his left arm following a car accident. Thinking he would never drum again, Allen became sad and depressed.

However, his bandmates had other ideas and encouraged him to find a new way to continue playing the drums as he had done since he was nine years old.

With the help of his friends, such as Def Leppard lead singer Joe Elliot and fellow drummer Jeff Rich, Allen began working on a special electronic drum kit with a company called Simmons. The equipment was the first of its kind and allowed him to play using only his right hand and both his feet.

Allen has said a turning point for him was receiving letters from fans worldwide. This, plus the support of his family, friends, and bandmates, gave him the encouragement he needed to get behind the drums and do what he loved once more.

IN 1986, LESS THAN TWO YEARS AFTER HIS ACCIDENT, ALLEN GOT BACK ON STAGE AND DELIVERED A BLISTERING PERFORMANCE AT THE MONSTERS OF ROCK FESTIVAL.

The following year, the band released Hysteria, their first album since Allen's accident. It became the most successful album of their career, with over 20 million copies sold across the globe.

Allen still plays for Def Leppard today, touring the world and enjoying a career that has lasted over 30 years with the band he started out with when he was just a teenager. In 2018, Def

Leppard was inducted into the Rock 'n Roll Hall of Fame in the US.

According to Allen, the accident changed his outlook on life forever. In his own words: "Before my accident, I was a little too…selfish and self-absorbed, and for me, to now be at the place where I can kinda give back and inspire people, I'm blessed. I'm really blessed."

After his accident and the experience of losing his arm, Allen suffered from depression. But coming through the other side of it gave him the desire to help others who have endured trauma as he has.

He founded a charity called the Raven Drum Foundation to help survivors of traumatic events come to terms with their experiences.

He also started the One Hand Drum Company, which raises funds for his foundation by selling merchandise, including signed pictures of "Stick Rick," an illustrated character he drew of himself, with the slogan "Life Is Great!! Be a Rockstar!"

While Allen talks openly about how losing his arm changed his life, he has never let his injury define him.

He is best known to his fans as the "Thunder God," a powerful, talented musician rather than an accident victim or someone with a disability.

Losing an arm can be a massive physical and emotional setback for any human being, especially if it can potentially stop you from making a living and doing what you love.

"If I couldn't play drums, it would have destroyed me," he said of the experience. "If you're thrown in the deep end, you swim, and that's basically what I did."

For Rick Allen, getting back behind the drums and deciding to overcome his physical limitations and persevere as a musician must have seemed like an impossible task.

Thanks to the power of courage, positive thinking, and hard work, his dream came true, and he could continue doing what he loved. His story serves as an inspiration to us all.

No matter what life throws your way – what obstacles or setbacks – remember that ANYTHING IS POSSIBLE if you set your mind to it and NEVER GIVE UP.

Nelson Mandela

POLITICIAN (1918 – 2013)

Nelson Mandela was a freedom fighter who spent 27 years in prison before becoming president of South Africa.

A WINNER is a DREAMER who NEVER gives up.

− Nelson Mandela

In May 1994, Nelson Mandela became South Africa's first president elected in fully democratic, multiracial elections. His inauguration was a proud moment for the country, but to get there, Mandela had to make many difficult sacrifices.

The year before he became president, Mandela won the Nobel Peace Prize alongside then President FW De Klerk, who was the last leader of what is known as the apartheid government. The two politicians worked together to end apartheid, an unfair political system that stripped South Africa's black majority of political power, wealth, land, human rights, and dignity.

Mandela devoted his life to fighting apartheid as a member of a political movement called the African National Congress (ANC). The ANC began as a peaceful movement that organized protests against apartheid. Because it opposed the government, the ANC was banned in 1960.

In response, Mandela was one of the members of the ANC who felt more radical action needed to be taken. He helped establish the ANC's militant wing, uMkhonto we Sizwe ("the spear of the nation"), which led a campaign of sabotage against the apartheid government.

Because of this, Mandela had to go underground, becoming a fugitive and traveling across Africa to meet many of the continent's political leaders. Upon his return to South Africa in 1962, he was arrested. He spent the next 27 years of his life in jail.

DESPITE SPENDING ALMOST **THREE DECADES** STRIPPED OF HIS FREEDOM FOR FIGHTING AN UNJUST SYSTEM, **WHEN** HE WAS **RELEASED** FROM PRISON, **MANDELA WAS NOT ANGRY** OR BITTER.

Instead, he spoke of a peaceful transition from apartheid to genuine democracy and reconciliation between white and black South Africans. Some believe that, without his influence, there might have been a South African civil war when apartheid ended.

While he ultimately became a global symbol of freedom and justice, Nelson Mandela began his life in Mvezo, a small, rural village in the hills of South Africa's Eastern Cape.

Born in July 1918, Mandela was a member of the Thembu royal family, who speak Xhosa, the second most widely spoken native language in South Africa. He had fond memories of his childhood, which he spent herding cattle and playing with his friends.

His royal upbringing allowed Mandela access to something unavailable to many black South Africans at the time—an education at Fort Hare, the country's only university that admitted black students. Before finishing his studies, Mandela left for South Africa's biggest city, the bustling, fast-paced Johannesburg.

There, he eventually gained enough education to be able to practice law. He started the first law firm in South Africa, founded by black partners in 1952 with his friend Oliver Tambo, who would become one of his closest allies in the anti-apartheid struggle.

Apartheid was a political system designed to benefit South Africa's white minority at the expense of its other groups. The system divided the country into four races — white, black, colored, and Indian/Asian — with only white South Africans enjoying freedom. Despite making up the majority of the population, any South African who wasn't white was not allowed to vote or have a say in the future of their country.

The freedom of black South Africans was also limited by the many unjust laws of apartheid. These limited where black people were allowed to live, what they were allowed to own, what beaches they could step on, what benches they could sit on, who they could marry, and many other things.

Fighting this system took a lot of bravery, as the apartheid government would not tolerate opposition, and devoting one's life to being a freedom fighter meant spending it in jail or on the run. In Mandela's case, he spent nearly 30 years of his life in prison, many of them in the notorious Robben Island Prison.

HE WAS FINALLY RELEASED FROM PRISON IN 1990, AND IN 1994 HE WAS ELECTED PRESIDENT OF SOUTH AFRICA IN THE COUNTRY'S FIRST FREE ELECTION.

He served as president until 1999 and became a global peace ambassador.

In his autobiography, Long Walk to Freedom, Mandela wrote about courage:

"I LEARNED THAT COURAGE WAS NOT THE ABSENCE OF FEAR, BUT THE TRIUMPH OVER IT. THE BRAVE MAN IS NOT HE WHO DOES NOT FEEL AFRAID, BUT HE WHO CONQUERS THAT FEAR."

Positive thinking also played a massive role in Mandela's life. Instead of feeling anger and resentment towards those who had imprisoned him for so long, he focused on what was best for his country. He focused on his dream of a peaceful transition from apartheid to democracy.

Mandela never gave up on his ultimate goal — freedom for the people of South Africa. The fact that he harnessed the courage and positivity within to achieve this goal reminds us of how important it is to never give up on what you believe in.

Perhaps Mandela himself said it best:

"IT ALWAYS SEEMS IMPOSSIBLE UNTIL IT'S DONE."

Pelé

SOCCER PLAYER (1940-PRESENT)

Brazil's Pelé rose from poverty to become the greatest soccer player of all time.

COURAGE can bring HUGE BENEFITS to those who are PREPARED.

- Pelé

The man the world would soon know as Pelé began his life in October 1940 as Edson Arantes do Nascimento. He was born in the Brazilian city of Três Corações, where his father was a soccer player, inspiring Pelé's passion for what he liked to call "the beautiful game."

Growing up, Pelé's family couldn't afford a soccer ball. Together with a group of young friends nicknamed "the shoeless ones," he made do with whatever he could find. Sometimes they'd practice with a sock stuffed with newspaper, while other times, they used a grapefruit.

What Pelé lacked in equipment, he made up for with passion, and he was soon playing for several amateur teams. He also played futsal, a form of indoor soccer, which helped him hone his skills. Futsal is a faster game than soccer, and Pelé says it taught him to make lightning-quick decisions on the pitch.

The coach of one of his amateur teams, Waldemar De Brito, recognized Pelé's talent and encouraged him to try out for the professional soccer club Santos FC. He told them that Pelé was no ordinary player. In fact, he predicted the young man would one day become the "greatest player in the world."

Pelé's rise to fame was swift. He made his professional debut for Santos FC at 15, becoming the top goalscorer in the league within a year. In 1958, when he was 17, he became the youngest player to compete in the World Cup. Pelé broke another record when Brazil got to the finals and yet another when they beat Sweden 5-3, with the help of two goals from the teenage wonder himself.

After this display, many of the world's top soccer clubs, including Real Madrid, Inter Milan, Manchester United, and Juventus, tried to sign Pelé. The Brazilian President at the time, Jânio Quadros, was not very popular, and his people were scared the country would lose Pelé to a European soccer club. To gain popularity, Quadros passed a law declaring Pelé a national treasure.

This may sound like a nice gesture, but it made it illegal for Pelé to be transferred to an international club. For this reason, the best part of Pelé's career as a soccer player was spent entirely in his own country, at his first professional club, Santos FC. If this bothered Pelé, he never let it show. When asked why he didn't take any overseas opportunities, he would smile and say that he never considered leaving the club in his prime.

Pelé scored 77 goals for his national team, a record that stood until 2021 when Cristiano Ronaldo surpassed it for Portugal. Many of Pelé's other records still stand today. He's the only player to have won three World Cups with his country, and he has scored the most goals of any player for Brazil, as well as the most hat tricks (when a player scores three goals in one match), with a total of 92.

But Pelé was no glory-hunter. He recognized soccer as a team sport and holds the record for the most assists in the history of the World Cup.

Not just a great goalscorer and goal-provider, Pelé also had a beautiful playing style. "The ambition should always be to play an elegant game," he said in his autobiography.

Pelé's style was acrobatic and exciting, like all great Brazilian soccer players. He could play with both feet, had incredible skill in the air, and his close control and dribbling skills were outstanding. Many professional soccer players, commentators, and fans still consider him the greatest player of all time.

After retirement from professional soccer, Pelé became a global ambassador for "the beautiful game."

Pelé didn't believe that people are born great soccer players; instead, he felt that becoming one was more about attitude than natural skill. He said that his love of soccer and all the practice, hard work, and sacrifice made him a great success rather than just his talent.

A great example of how courage and positive thinking can lead to success, Pelé demonstrates that you can transcend poverty to reach the highest of heights.

If you find what you love and, like Pelé, pursue it with passion, you, too, can leave a blueprint of greatness for others to follow one day.

Over to You

What incredible stories of courage and determination!

It takes a lot of courage to pursue a dream, especially when the odds are against you. But all four people in this chapter exemplify this in their own way.

Jaylen Arnold stood up to his bullies. Rick Allen didn't let his disability stop him from playing the drums. Nelson Mandela never gave up on his fight for equality. And Pelé pursued his dream of becoming a professional soccer player, despite growing up in poverty. All four of these people faced adversity but didn't let it stop them from achieving their dreams.

That's an important lesson. Never give up on your dreams, regardless of what life throws at you.

Activity - Courage Collage

What does courage mean to you? Create a collage or drawing that represents courage to you. Include words and images that inspire you.

For example, your collage could include images of people who have inspired you with their acts of courage, words that describe courage to you, or pictures of things you are afraid of and want to overcome. Be creative! There are no wrong answers.

When you're finished, share your collage with someone and explain what it means to you.

And finally, use the collage as a reminder...

YOU ARE CAPABLE OF ANYTHING YOU SET YOUR MIND TO!

Courage Collage

Add drawings, quotes or write about people you admire or who motivate you. They could be friends, family or famous people who have shown courage.

COURAGE IS

Standing up to bullies

My Hero

CHAPTER 2

SELF-BELIEF AND THE MINDSET OF A WINNER

BELIEVE
you CAN
and you're
HALFWAY
there.

— Theodore Roosevelt

Whatever you want to achieve in life, it all starts with self-belief.

Do you want to make the football team? Or perhaps you want to get straight A's or someday start your own business? Whatever it is, you need to believe that you can do it and have what it takes. Only then will you be able to achieve great things.

But what exactly is self-belief?

Self-belief is the foundation of success. It's having faith in your own abilities. It's knowing that you can do something, even if you haven't done it before. It allows you to persevere when things get tough and keep going when everyone else has given up.

SELF-BELIEF IS A MINDSET THAT SAYS,
"I CAN DO THIS."

When you have that belief, anything is possible. You'll be more likely to take risks and more resilient when things don't go as planned.

If you want to be successful, you need to have the mindset of a winner. You need to believe in yourself and your abilities.

As the people in the stories below will show you, anything is possible when you have that belief.

David Goggins

NAVY SEAL & ATHLETE (1975 – PRESENT)

Former US Navy SEAL David Goggins overcame a life of hardship to become a world-famous ultramarathon runner, a triathlete, and one of the fittest men on the planet.

GREATNESS pulls MEDIOCRITY into the mud. GET OUT THERE and GET AFTER IT.

— David Goggins

When David Goggins first tried becoming a Navy SEAL in 2001, the recruiters laughed at him. Trained to fight in the sea, in the air, and on land, US Navy SEALs are an elite special operations force. To become a SEAL, you must endure one of the most challenging training programs in the world. Only 200 out of every 1,000 people who try to become Navy SEALs succeed.

Goggins weighed 300 pounds at the time, and the odds were very much against him.

But Goggins was determined to turn his life around, so when he realized he'd need to lose at least 100 pounds to join the US Navy, he harnessed all of his mental and physical strength to make this happen. After reaching his goal weight in under three months, he was given the opportunity to train to become a Navy SEAL.

Goggins progressed in the Navy SEAL training program until he got to Hell Week, an infamous test of endurance where trainees complete 130 hours of grueling exercises on very little sleep. On his first attempt, he contracted pneumonia. On his second try, he was forced to quit after developing a stress fracture. If he wanted to continue his training, he only had one more opportunity to pass.

Knowing that he needed to strength-en his mind and body, Goggins developed his philosophy of mental toughness, which saw him conquer his fears and limits to achieve physical greatness. As he says:

"WHEN YOUR MIND IS TELLING YOU THAT YOU'RE DONE, THAT YOU'RE EXHAUSTED, THAT YOU CANNOT POSSIBLY GO ANY FURTHER, YOU'RE ONLY ACTUALLY 40% DONE."

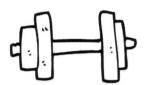

Thanks to this change in mindset, he passed Hell Week on the third attempt.

Goggins was a US Navy SEAL for 20 years. He served in Iraq and Afghanistan and was awarded several prestigious medals and honors for his work in the military, including the prestigious "Top Enlisted Man" award.

His transformation from decorated soldier to ultramarathon runner resulted from tragedy. In 2005, a helicopter crash led to the death of some of his closest friends and fellow soldiers. To honor them, Goggins began a journey that saw him raise over $2 million for charity through long-distance running. He eventually became one of the world's best endurance athletes.

Today, Goggins is known as one of the fittest people on earth. He has broken records and won awards not only as an ultra-marathon runner but also as a triathlete. But to get to this level, he had to face and overcome poverty, prejudice, and physical abuse while growing up.

Goggins' decision to master his mental and physical strength was not motivated by a desire for the awards or fame he'd later attain but by wanting to overcome his fears. One of those fears was his own father, who was aggressive and violent towards Goggins and his mother when he was young. Goggins also wanted to overcome the voice in his head telling him he wasn't good enough, caused by years of bullying at school.

Goggins' struggles didn't end after he started achieving his physical goals. In 2010, he was diagnosed with a condition called an atrial septal defect. The doctor had spotted a small hole in his heart that had been there since birth and kept it from being able to function at full capacity. He had also put a severe physical strain on himself in his transformation from an overweight, inactive young man to an athletic powerhouse.

So, Goggins started a new physical challenge to rehabilitate himself and save his own life. Gradually, a strict regime of stretching and physical therapy allowed his heart and other organs to heal, and he could continue competing as an athlete.

According to Goggins, he owes his success to his "day one, week one" strategy. This means never getting too comfortable and always making as much effort as you would on that first day of a new job. Another part of his philosophy is the 40% Rule, which

stems from his belief that most human beings only function at 40% of their true capabilities and can learn to unlock their genuine potential.

In 2018, Goggins was able to share this philosophy, as well as the story of how he overcame the struggles of his upbringing, in his book, "Can't Hurt Me: Master Your Mind and Defy the Odds," which became a bestseller and has sold over 2.5 million copies to date.

Goggins' story reminds us of the importance of mentally and physically challenging ourselves. While he didn't start out with the mindset of a winner, he was able to transform himself through the power of self-belief, proving that anyone can do the same.

BELIEVING IN YOURSELF AND MASTERING YOUR MINDSET IS ALL IT TAKES TO OVERCOME ANY CHALLENGE AND ACHIEVE ANYTHING YOU SET OUT TO DO.

David Goggins is living proof of that.

Jim Carrey

ACTOR (1962 – PRESENT)

Jim Carrey is a comedian and one of Hollywood's
most successful actors.

Life opens up opportunities to you, and you either TAKE THEM or you STAY afraid of TAKING them.

- Jim Carrey

Jim Carrey's life is a true rags-to-riches story. From sleeping in a van with his family to becoming one of Hollywood's most successful actors, Carrey has achieved massive success.

Born January 17, 1962, as James Eugene Carrey in Newmarket, Ontario, Canada, he was the youngest of four children. By age eight, he had already discovered his talent for making impressions of people when he started making faces in front of the mirror. Around this time, his interest in performing emerged after his teacher asked him to perform his routine for the Christmas assembly. The thin boy with the chipped front tooth was a success.

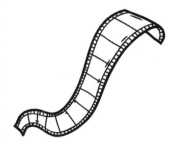

The following year, when Carrey was nine, the family moved to Burlington, where he attended a local school. Carrey had dyslexia but learned to compensate by developing a phenomenal memory that would serve him well in later years. While Carrey attended junior high, one of his teachers allowed him time at the end of each day to perform stand-up routines for his classmates — on the condition that he did his work and behaved well.

CARREY'S FAMILY STRUGGLED FINANCIALLY, AND WHEN HIS DAD LOST HIS JOB, THEY ENDED UP LIVING IN A YELLOW VW CAMPER VAN.

They would travel between campgrounds and parking lots, living off whatever his dad could earn as a musician. But to young Jim Carrey, rather than being a difficult time, this was an adventure in which he was always on the move and constantly learning new things.

Eventually, after his dad got a job as an accountant at a factory, things settled down, and the family moved into a house owned by the factory. To help support the family, Jim Carrey and his brother would attend school during the day and work as janitors at the factory at night. He eventually quit high school when he turned 16 in 1978.

During this time, Carrey started developing his skills as a comedian, performing stand-up at local clubs. In 1983, he moved to Hollywood to pursue his dream of becoming a comedian.

This was a risk for young Carrey, with only a grade nine education, but it paid off in more ways than one. He secured a gig at the Comedy Store within weeks of arriving in LA. He also attracted the attention of comedy legend Rodney Dangerfield, who was so impressed by the youngster that he asked him to go on tour with him as his opening act. From then on, there was no looking back.

In 1988, he made a memorable appearance in the Clint Eastwood film "The Dead Pool." After that, there was no stopping him as he went on to star in Fox television's comedy hit "In Living Color" and his first TV show "Jim Carrey's Unnatural Act," which premiered to rave reviews.

Carrey's star was on the rise in Hollywood. In 1994, he returned to movies, landing the lead role in the comedy "Ace Ventura: Pet Detective," which catapulted him to stardom. He went on to star in a string of successful movies, including "The Mask," "Dumb and Dumber," "Batman Forever" (as the Riddler), and "Liar, Liar." In 1998, he picked up his first Golden Globe award for best actor in "The Truman Show."

Carrey had arrived – and he was only
GETTING STARTED.

Carrey's road to fame and fortune has not always been easy. Like everyone, he has had to endure tough times and face obstacles, but he worked hard and never lost sight of his goal. He knew what he wanted to do with his life and persevered until he achieved it.

Just like Jim Carrey, you can overcome life's obstacles and succeed. Use adversity to gain experience and grow, and use what you have learned to achieve your goals.

WITH THE RIGHT MINDSET AND DETERMINATION, ANYTHING IS POSSIBLE, NO MATTER THE ODDS AGAINST YOU.

Muhammad Ali

BOXER (1942 – 2016)

Muhammed Ali was an American boxer, philanthropist, and social activist. He is considered one of the greatest heavyweight boxers of all time.

IMPOSSIBLE
is **NOT** *a* fact.
It's an opinion...

IMPOSSIBLE

is nothing.

- Muhammad Ali

From the deep south of America to the world stage of boxing, Muhammed Ali's life was an incredible achievement.

Born Cassius Marcellus Clay Jr. on January 17, 1942, in Louisville, Kentucky, Ali was a shy, skinny child who struggled with reading and was often teased by other kids. Growing up in racially segregated America at a time when black people were discriminated against and not allowed to eat in the same restaurants, attend the same schools, or even sit together on public transport with whites, he soon developed a sensitivity to injustice.

But an event in 1954 would prove pivotal in young Ali's life. At age 12, he and a friend rode their bicycles to the Louisville Home Show, lured by the prospect of free candy and popcorn. Unfortunately, Ali's bike was stolen. Distraught, he approached a police officer, Joe Martin, who was on duty that day. Unbeknownst to Ali, this meeting would change his life forever.

As Martin later recalled: "He was crying and sobbing, saying how he was going to whup whoever stole his bike. I said, 'Well, you better learn how to fight before you start challenging people.'"

And so, Ali started boxing lessons. At first, since he was inexperienced, many of the other boys beat him in the ring. But there was one thing they had not counted on — Ali's dedication and determination to succeed. Every day he showed up for lessons and put in the hard work. Soon he was training six days a week, perfecting the moves he was taught.

By 16, Ali had overcome his shyness. To boost his confidence, he often bragged to the other fighters that they couldn't beat him. He still lost the odd fight but was the winner more times than not, which got him noticed by boxing fans around the county.

During this time, Ali dropped out of high school to concentrate on qualifying for the upcoming Olympics in Rome in 1960. But there was one problem: He would have to go to California to qualify, which meant flying to get there. Ali was afraid of flying, but the determination to succeed won out. He flew to California, won his trials, and made the Olympic team.

At that time, Ali wasn't heavy enough to enter the Olympics as a heavyweight, so he entered the light heavyweight division. Despite a fierce battle in the ring in his gold medal match, he won. At just 18 years old, Ali was the Olympic champion.

When he returned home to the United States, he turned professional. He took on opponents for the next four years and won every match. Still, he appeared to lack true knockout power until his match against Sonny Liston in February 1964 for the heavyweight world title. In a stunning upset, Ali became the new world champion. Two days later, he shocked the world of boxing when he announced that he had accepted the teachings of the Nation of Islam and would now be known as

Muhammad Ali rather than Cassius Clay. The next three years saw him dominate heavyweight boxing, but other events outside the ring would soon rock his world.

In April 1967, at the height of the Vietnam War, Ali refused to be drafted into the US military on religious grounds. This action cost him dearly. He was stripped of all his world titles and banned from boxing. But Ali didn't give up. He continued to speak out against the war and fight for his beliefs, even though it meant he couldn't box for over three years.

In 1971, he was finally allowed to return to the ring, but the four years of being out of action had taken their toll. During his absence, Joe Frazier had become the new heavyweight champion, and Ali lost his first-ever professional fight.

Digging deep, Ali, who was now 29 years old, painstakingly and determinedly worked his way back to claim the world heavyweight title in 1974 against George Foreman in the "Rumble in the Jungle" in Kinshasa, Zaire (now the Democratic Republic of Congo).

It was one of the most significant sporting events of all time, with an estimated 1 billion people watching on television. Ali pulled off one of the greatest upsets in boxing history, knocking out Foreman in the eighth round to become the world heavyweight champion again.

With a final record of 56 wins and five losses with 37 knockouts, Ali retired from the ring at age 39 in 1981. But it was not only his career as a professional boxer that inspired people; it was also his fight for racial equality. Throughout his life, Ali became a unifying force for Americans of all races, using his fame to highlight suffering worldwide and advocate for peace.

Muhammad Ali was an extraordinary man who overcame tremendous obstacles to achieve his dreams. He came from a humble background and achieved greatness through hard work, determination, and a never-give-up attitude.

Ali once said:

"You could be the world's best garbage man, the world's best model; IT DON'T MATTER WHAT YOU DO IF YOU'RE THE BEST."

The point is that anything is possible with the right mindset and the determination to put in the hard work. As Ali taught us, if you get knocked down by one of life's experiences, learn from it and stand up to fight another day.

Sir Mo Farah

ATHLETE (1983 – PRESENT)

Somali-born Sir Mo Farah overcame a tragic childhood to become the UK's greatest distance runner.

> ⁓ Don't **DREAM**
> of **WINNING.**
> **TRAIN** for it. ⁓
>
> — Mo Farah

Sir Mohamed Muktar Jama Farah, better known as Mo Farah to his fans, was born Hussein Abdi Kahin in the African country of Somalia in May 1983.

With an early life disrupted by war and poverty, few would have guessed that he would one day become one of the world's greatest distance runners.

Farah's four Olympic medals and six world titles make him the most successful distance runner ever. He rose above his circumstances by believing in himself to achieve fantastic success.

While his dream as a high school student in England was to play soccer for Arsenal or become a car mechanic, his physical education teacher soon identified Farah's true calling—running.

He was soon winning school titles and showing signs of brilliance on the track. In 2001, he won the European Junior 5,000 meters. But his career really picked up after winning the European Cross Country Championships and a silver medal in the 5,000 meters at the European Track and Field Championships.

In 2008, Farah had the opportunity to train in Kenya and Ethiopia, and in 2010 he won the "double" at the European Championship, taking home gold medals for the 5,000 and 10,000 meters. He also broke a British record, becoming the first UK runner to complete the 5,000 meters in under 13 minutes.

But Farah was just getting started. In 2011, his career went into overdrive. He became the first UK runner to become world champion in the 5,000 meters and broke the record for the 10,000 meters at the European Championships.

In 2012, he won his (and Britain's) first 10,000-meter Olympic gold medal while also taking home the gold for the 5,000 meters. He continued on this path, becoming the most successful runner in European Athletics Championship history after winning his fifth title in 2014.

In 2016, Farah captured what is known as the double-double by winning both the 5,000- and 10,000-meter races in two consecutive Olympics Games. It was a fitting end to the career of an athletic superstar. In 2017, not long after winning his 10th world title, he hung up his running shoes and retired. In the same year, he was knighted by Queen Elizabeth II for services to athletics.

Farah's achievements are even more remarkable considering the extreme adversity he had to overcome. In a 2022 documentary, "The Real Mo Farah," he revealed that the original story he'd given about his journey from Somalia to Britain was false. He was afraid to tell the real story for a long time. He was brought to the UK through human trafficking — when people are illegally sent to another country against their will.

Farah's father sadly died in the Somali Civil War when the runner was only four years old. While living with an uncle in Djibouti, he was flown to England without his mother's knowledge.

Next, Farah was given the false name he still uses to this day and forced to work as a servant, only getting the chance to attend school from the age of 12. He confided in his running coach about his situation and was eventually able to move in with a Somali family, ending his life of servitude.

Farah was reunited with his birth mother, Aisha, for the first time in a decade in 2000, when a tape she made of her singing, with a phone number on it, reached him. They have remained in contact ever since.

The importance of self-belief in Sir Mo Farah's story can't be understated. As he once said,

"IT HAS BEEN A LONG JOURNEY, BUT IF YOU DREAM AND HAVE THE AMBITION AND WANT TO WORK HARD, THEN YOU CAN ACHIEVE. IT DOESN'T JUST COME OVERNIGHT, YOU'VE GOT TO TRAIN FOR IT AND BELIEVE IN YOURSELF; THAT'S THE MOST IMPORTANT THING. LOOK AT MY SUCCESS."

Sir Mo Farah didn't let the trauma of his childhood or the tragedy of his situation stop him from believing in himself and thinking like a winner.

If you sometimes wonder how you can make your dreams a reality, think of his story and remember that there are two things you'll need to get there: self-belief and the mindset of a winner.

Over to You

David Goggins, Jim Carrey, Muhammad Ali, and Mo Farah are all very different men who have achieved success in different ways. Still, there are some key things that they all have in common. One of those things is self-belief.

They believed that they could achieve anything they set their mind to.

Instead of looking at OBSTACLES as IMPOSSIBLE TO OVERCOME, THEY SAW THEM AS CHALLENGES TO BE CONQUERED.

They didn't let their limitations hold them back — they used them as motivation to push themselves harder.

And because of that, they achieved things that others thought were impossible.

So, how do you develop self-belief?

Start by setting realistic goals for yourself. Then, take small steps to achieve those goals. As you start seeing results, your self-belief will grow.

Finally, surround yourself with positive people who support your dreams and will help you stay motivated.

When you combine self-belief with a winner's mindset, anything is possible.

Activity - The Power of Yet

One way to develop self-belief is to change how you think about obstacles.

Instead of looking at them as impossible to overcome, see them as challenges to be conquered.

This activity will help you do that.

If you've started something new or there's something you really want to achieve, instead of thinking, **"I CAN'T DO THIS,"** try saying, **"I CAN'T DO THIS YET."**

For example, if you're learning to play the piano, instead of thinking, "I'm not good at this," say, "I'm not good at this YET."

If you're trying to improve your math, instead of thinking, "This is too hard," say, "I'm not good at this YET."

JUST BECAUSE YOU CAN'T DO SOMETHING YET DOESN'T MEAN YOU NEVER WILL BE ABLE TO DO IT.

By adding the word "yet," you're telling yourself that you CAN do it. It's just a matter of time and practice. And as you start seeing results, your self-belief will grow.

Give this a try on the next page! And the next time you're feeling doubtful, remind yourself that you can't do it YET, then see how your mindset starts to change.

The Power of YET

I am not good at singing

YET

YET

YET

YET

YET

CHAPTER 3

NEVER GIVING UP & BEATING THE ODDS

If you fall behind, run faster. NEVER GIVE UP, NEVER SURRENDER, and RISE UP. against the odds.

— Jesse Jackson

Most people give up when things get tough.

They quit when they don't see results right away. But successful people are the ones who never give up. They keep going, even when it's hard, and they don't let anything or anyone stop them from achieving their goals.

It's like running a marathon. You can't expect to cross the finish line if you give up halfway through. You need to keep going, even when your legs are tired and you want to stop because if you never give up, you'll eventually reach your goal.

NEVER GIVING UP IS WHAT SEPARATES THE SUCCESSFUL FROM THE UNSUCCESSFUL.

So, how do you become someone who never gives up?

YOU NEED TO HAVE A LOT OF DETERMINATION AND PERSEVERANCE.

YOU NEED TO BE WILLING TO WORK HARD, EVEN WHEN IT'S TOUGH.

And you need to never give up on your dreams, no matter what — as the people in the stories below will show you.

Sir Ernest Shackleton

EXPLORER (1874 – 1922)

Sir Ernest Shackleton was a famous explorer who
led three British expeditions to Antarctica.

DIFFICULTIES
are just THINGS to
OVERCOME,
after all.

- Ernest Shackleton

Imagine being trapped in an ice floe for nine months with no hope of rescue. Surrounded by nothing but darkness and cold, your only chance of survival is to keep your head up and find a way to escape.

This was the reality for Ernest Shackleton and his crew during their ill-fated expedition to Antarctica in 1915.

Born in Kilkea, County Kildare, Ireland, on February 15, 1874, Shackleton was the second of 10 children.

His early life was shaped by two main influences: his family's strong religious faith and his father's love of adventure. These influences would stay with him throughout his life.

Growing up, Shackleton and his siblings were taught to swim in the nearby river. They were also put on horseback early on by their dad, who encouraged them to be afraid of nothing. Shackleton was also a keen reader, fascinated by stories of buried treasure and adventure, which would shape his life in later years.

At 10 years old, Shackleton made his first voyage across the Irish Sea when his family moved to England. It was here that he first attended school, having been home-schooled by a gov-erness up until that point. Although he was encouraged by his dad to follow in his footsteps as a doctor, Shackleton rebelled, not wanting a routine but longing instead for freedom and adventure. Instead, at just 16 years of age, he left school. He took an apprenticeship in the Merchant Navy, where he rose through the ranks until qualifying as a master mariner in 1898.

While serving on the ship "Tintagel Castle," Shackleton first heard about the proposed National Antarctic Expedition being planned under Captain Robert Scott's command. There and then, he made up his mind he was going to be a part of it. When

Captain Scott's ship "Discovery" set sail for Antarctica in 1901, Shackleton was onboard as the third lieutenant.

The ship ended up becoming stranded in Antarctica, locked in by the ice for two years. During this time, Shackleton joined a sled party over the Ross Ice Shelf with Captain Scott and  Edward Wilson. They established a new record as being closest to the South Pole. Unfortunately, Shackleton was ultimately beset by bad health. He was removed from duty and sent home on a supply ship in 1903.

Back in England, it wasn't long before Shackleton became restless. His trip to Antarctica had stirred something within him. He wanted to reach the South Pole. So, in 1907, at age 33 and funded by private loans, Shackleton set out on the "Nimrod" on what was known as the British Antarctic Expedition. Unfortunately, his goal of reaching the South Pole eluded him. Still, his trip attracted widespread interest and made him a national hero, earning him a knighthood from King Edward VII.

The race for the South Pole ended three years later in 1911, when Roald Amundsen, a fellow explorer, reached the South Pole, followed closely by Captain Scott. But Shackleton was not to be put off. Instead, he resolved to set a new record by crossing Antarctica from sea to sea via the South Pole in what was to be known as the Imperial Trans-Antarctic Expedition.

In August 1914, he set off from London to Antarctica with a crew of 27 men. Just months into the voyage, disaster struck when his ship, the "Endurance," had its first encounter with an ice pack and became frozen into the heavy ice.

By September, the pressure on the ship from the ice had become too much. Shackleton ordered his men to abandon it and set up camp on the ice.

IN NOVEMBER 1915, THE "ENDURANCE" SANK BELOW THE ICE INTO THE FRIGID WATERS, LEAVING SHACKLETON AND HIS CREW STRANDED WITH NO MEANS OF COMMUNICATING WITH THE OUTSIDE WORLD.

What followed next is a testament to Shackleton's bravery, determination, and never-give-up attitude.

HE KNEW THE ONLY WAY TO SAVE HIS CREW WAS TO kEEP GOING, NO MATTER WHAT.

So, Shackleton and his men embarked on a journey across the Antarctic continent, enduring some of the harshest conditions on Earth. First, all 27 crew members used lifeboats to sail to Elephant Island. But Elephant Island was remote and uninhabited, so Shackleton knew he had to find a way to get help.

He set off with five of his men in a 20-foot open boat in a desperate attempt to reach the island of South Georgia. The trip was painfully slow and grueling through the rough seas, and frostbite was beginning to affect their exposed fingers and hands in the constant cold. But after 16 days, having traveled over 700 miles by sea, they reached the southern coast of South Georgia.

Unfortunately, their ordeal was not over yet. Shackleton and his men still had to hike across the island's mountains to reach the nearest settlement. The journey was long and arduous; the men only had 50 feet of rope and basic clothes. But they eventually arrived at a whaling station on May 20, 1916.

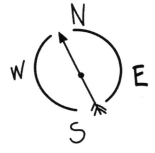

From here, Shackleton arranged a rescue mission for his men still on Elephant Island. After three failed attempts due to the sea icing up, he eventually managed to rescue the rest of his crew in August 1916.

Incredibly, despite the hardship and danger, they had faced, not a single life was lost.

Shackleton returned home to a hero's welcome but once again soon became restless for adventure. In September 1921, at the age of 47, he set off for Antarctica on the Shackleton-Rowett Expedition, joined by many of his former crew members from the "Endurance." Unfortunately, this was his last voyage. He suffered a heart attack on January 5, 1922, and died after arriving in South Georgia, in Antarctica.

Throughout his life, Shackleton never gave up pursuing his dreams, no matter what obstacles he faced. This attitude, courage, determination, and perseverance he and his crew displayed on the expedition inspire us all.

LIKE SHACKLETON, YOU SHOULD NEVER GIVE UP ON PURSUING AND ACHIEVING THE GOALS YOU HAVE SET FOR YOURSELF.

With the right mindset and determination to succeed, you can power your way through disappointments and find a way to overcome the obstacles you face in life. If Shackleton could do it all those years ago, so can you.

Iqbal Masih

CHILDREN'S RIGHTS ACTIVIST (1983 – 1995)

Iqbal Masih was a Pakistani children's rights activist and former child laborer.

CHILDREN should have PENS in their hands, NOT TOOLS.

- Iqbal Masih

Iqbal Masih's story is a powerful one of courage, bravery, and determination to never give up the fight for freedom for child laborers.

Born in 1983 in Muridke, a commercial area near Lahore, Pakistan, his actual date of birth was not recorded. Growing up, the young boy was surrounded by poverty, which was made worse when his dad abandoned the family, leaving only his mom to take care of them.

In 1986, when Masih was just four years old, his mom, who worked as a housecleaner, borrowed 12 dollars from a local carpet weaving business owner to pay for his older brother's wedding. As the family was already deeply in debt, his mom took the loan out in Iqbal's name, which meant he was handed over to the business owner as bonded labor. From that day forward, his life changed forever. He was stripped of his childhood and forced to weave carpets until all the money, including interest and expenses, was paid back.

Working 14 hours a day, six days a week, in often sweltering and cramped conditions at the carpet weaving factory, Masih often endured beatings and whipping whenever his work slowed. There was little hope of him ever attaining his freedom and paying off his family's loan, as, after the costs of his apprenticeship, food, tools, and fines for his mistakes, the two cents per day he earned did not cover it all. The outlook was bleak for the young boy.

For five long years, Masih toiled in the carpet weaving factory until one day, he and some other children seized an opportunity and escaped, hoping they could report their employer to the nearest police station for beating them. Unfortunately, the police returned them to the factory owner, demanding a finder's fee for returning escaped bonded laborers.

 Masih found himself back where he had started, but this didn't stop him from attempting another escape at age 10, this time to a Freedom Day celebration of the Brick Layers Union. It was here that he met the man who was to be an instrumental force in his life and set him on a different path that would see thousands of enslaved children break free from slavery. That man was Ehsaan Ullah Khan, an activist who opposed slavery and child labor in Pakistan. Appalled by Masih's story, Ehsaan set about freeing the boy and the other children from the carpet weaving factory. He also helped secure his admission to the Bonded Labor Liberation Fund (BLLF) school.

Masih had never attended school, but he was a bright student and a quick learner and completed four years of education in only two years. At school, he interacted with social activists who greatly influenced his understanding of labor laws and human rights. He was adamant that he would become a lawyer and help eradicate child bondage labor in developing nations such as Pakistan.

But it didn't end there. Encouraged by the BLFF, he gave speeches during his two years at school about the horrors he and the other children had experienced at the carpet-weaving factory. As Masih's popularity grew, he spoke out against enslaved children and bonded laborers at demonstrations across Pakistan with greater confidence, educating slave laborers and encouraging them to escape. In that year alone, it is estimated that some 3,000 children escaped their owners after hearing Masih speak. His rising popularity, however, did not sit well with the organized business mafias that dominated the communities. He was considered a threat to business.

Masih's story came to the world's attention. In October 1994, at age 11, he was invited to the United States to receive the Reebok Human Rights Award with his mentor Ehsaan. Stopping off in Stockholm, Sweden, on the way to the US, the young, frail boy captured the media's attention when he called for a boycott of Pakistani carpets to put pressure on the authorities in Pakistan.

But tragedy was about to strike. Back in Pakistan a couple of months later, on April 16, 1995, Masih, who had spent the day visiting his mom and family for Easter, decided to visit an uncle later that day with his two cousins. Unfortunately, that was the last time he was seen alive, as Masih was shot and killed. To this day, why he was killed remains a mystery, with the official police report claiming it was an accidental shooting by a local farmer.

Despite his short life, Masih took the courageous step of fighting for the rights of bonded laborers and enslaved children in Pakistan and around the world. Despite a life of pain and suffering, he never gave up on his mission to end child slavery by raising awareness and inspiring others to join in his efforts.

Like Iqbal Masih, you can make a difference in your life by believing in your dreams and never giving up on attaining them. Instead, stay focused and true to yourself, no matter your obstacles. It is by overcoming these obstacles and learning a lesson you become a stronger person.

Leonardo DiCaprio

ACTOR (1974 – PRESENT)

Leonardo DiCaprio is a well-known Hollywood actor, producer, and environmentalist.

Only YOU and YOU ALONE CAN CHANGE your SITUATION. DON'T BLAME it on ANYTHING or ANYONE.

- Leonardo DiCaprio

Leonardo DiCaprio has starred in some of the most popular movies of the past few decades, including "Titanic," "The Wolf of Wall Street," and "Inception." But DiCaprio is more than just a talented actor — he's also a committed environmentalist who has dedicated his time and energy to fighting climate change.

Born on November 11, 1974, in Los Angeles, California, Leonardo Wilhelm DiCaprio was an only child. His parents separated when he was one year old, but they were determined to raise their son together, so they moved into adjoining houses with a  shared garden in a downbeat suburb of Los Angeles. It was here, surrounded by crime and violence, that DiCaprio grew up.

It was an incident involving his stepbrother Adam Farrar that set DiCaprio on the path to stardom. Adam was 12 years old (three years older than Leo) and auditioned for a cornflakes commercial to earn some pocket money. He ended up doing 20 adverts and making $50,000. From that moment, DiCaprio made up his mind: He would escape his poor upbringing and become an actor, just like his stepbrother.

However, his first foray into acting did not go as planned. At age 11, DiCaprio tried to find the right agent to represent him but got turned down. Dejected, the young actor thought he had blown his chance, but this did not stop him from repeatedly trying to find an agent to take him on over the next three years. Unfortunately, no agent wanted to represent the short, skinny teenager. School was even worse. Although he liked to act tough, DiCaprio was constantly picked on and bullied.

Eventually, Farrar introduced DiCaprio to an agent, and he landed three acting roles in commercials. Things were finally looking up. But after this brief moment of fame, DiCaprio was back to being rejected by agents. One even suggested that he should change his name to Lenny Williams to make him more appealing to an American audience. He refused.

He continued to audition for parts for the next year and a half, only to be turned down. At that stage, DiCaprio wanted to quit. But then came the break he was looking for. He was signed up for commercials and minor roles in the Disney-produced Mickey's Safety club series. But he wanted more. He wanted to make a name for himself.

During this time, DiCaprio, who was not academically inclined, decided to drop out of high school and instead attend a free

local drama center. He was determined to get himself and his mom out of poverty. A significant turning point came in 1991 when he joined the cast of "Growing Pains" and made his debut with the horror movie "Critters 3," which he later described as "one of the worst films of all time." Still, he was determined and, above all, had the drive to succeed.

In the years that followed, he went on to star in several popular movies, including "What's Eating Gilbert Grape," "Romeo + Juliet," and "The Beach." But his role in the 1997 blockbuster "Titanic" made him a global superstar. "Titanic" was the highest-grossing movie of all time at that point and won 11 Academy Awards.

In recent years, DiCaprio has continued to act in hugely successful movies, including "Inception," "The Wolf of Wall Street," and "The Revenant," the latter of which won him his first Oscar.

But DiCaprio isn't just an actor—he's also a passionate environmentalist working to raise awareness about climate change and its effects on the planet. As a child, he first became aware of the rainforest's destruction while watching TV documentaries. This resonated with him and led to him becoming one of the most active celebrities to use their star power to raise awareness about climate change.

In 1998, he founded the Leonardo DiCaprio Foundation. His environmental organization works to protect vulnerable wildlife and ecosystems around the world. The foundation also supports projects that promote renewable energy and sustainability.

Through his work with the foundation, DiCaprio has helped to raise awareness of the importance of taking action on climate change. He has also been a vocal advocate for developing clean energy technologies.

In 2014, DiCaprio was named a United Nations Messenger of Peace, with a particular focus on climate change. This appointment recognizes his "long-standing commitment to environmental protection" and his efforts to "mobilize support for urgent action on climate change."

DiCaprio's work as an environmentalist proves that celebrities can use their platforms to make a difference in the world.

Leonardo DiCaprio's stardom certainly did not come easy in his early years. It took tenacity and determination to achieve his dream despite all the rejections he received at the time. Instead of giving up, he persevered, overcame the obstacles, and beat the odds by believing in himself.

LIKE DICAPRIO, YOU TOO MAY FACE REJECTION IN LIFE, BUT IT'S HOW YOU DEAL WITH IT THAT COUNTS. USE IT AS A LEARNING EXPERIENCE AND MOVE ON TOWARDS YOUR GOALS.

Never let anything stand in the way of achieving your dreams.

Jesse Owens

ATHLETE (1913 – 1980)

US sprinter Jesse Owens overcame the odds and rose to fame, winning four gold medals at the 1936 Olympics.

Find the GOOD.
It's ALL AROUND you.
FiND it,
SHOWCASE it,
and you'll START
BELIEVING IN it.

- Jesse Owens

The youngest of 10 children, James Cleveland "Jesse" Owens, was born into poverty in the small US community of Oakville, Alabama, in 1913.

Owens' family left for Cleveland, Ohio, when he was nine, as life was hard for African American families in the American South, where racial segregation — laws making it illegal for black and white people to coexist together, marry, or go to the same schools — were more severe than in other parts of the US.

When Owens started at his new school in Cleveland, a teacher asked what his name was and he answered, "J.C." His strong Southern accent made it sound like he was saying "Jesse," which became his new name.

Owens soon realized he had an unusual talent for running. In high school, he gained attention when he matched the world record of 9.4 seconds in the 100-yard dash and jumped 24 feet and 9.5 inches in the long jump at the national school championships.

His running skills became more legendary when he won eight championships at Ohio State University. And in 1935, in un-der an hour, he set three world records (for sprinting, the long jump, and hurdles) and tied for a fourth at the Big Ten athletics event in Michigan.

NO ONE SINCE THEN HAS MATCHED THIS INCREDIBLE ACHIEVEMENT. IT WAS CALLED "THE GREATEST 45 MINUTES EVER IN SPORTS" BY SPORTS ILLUSTRATED.

This fantastic display of athletic ability led to Owens competing in the 1936 Berlin Summer Olympics in Germany, where he won four gold medals.

His success at the Olympics in Germany was significant not just for him, but for the world, because of what it symbolized. He became the first athlete to win four gold medals at a single Olympic Games. And he achieved this remarkable feat while Germany's leader, Adolf Hitler, promoted his racist ideology.

 Hitler believed that white people were the master race, born mentally and physically superior and that everyone else was inferior. He was using the Olympic Games to showcase this belief to the world. But Owens' stunning victories and display of incredible athletic prowess completely shattered this myth.

At the same time that Germany was under the spell of Hitler's racist ideas, the US also had a long way to go on the road to racial equality. To understand the challenges Owens had to overcome to rise to the top of his field, one must look at what the US was like for African Americans when he was growing up.

Owens was the grandson of an enslaved person, and his father was a sharecropper, working in conditions that weren't much better than those enslaved people had endured.

Although slavery had been abolished in 1865, black people in America still faced many restrictions. They were not treated equally to white people. Owens trained for the Olympics during the "Segregation Era," when black Americans were legally prevented from being in the same areas and using the same services as white people. They were segregated in schools, restaurants, buses, and even drinking fountains.

In some US states, it was even against the law for black and white athletes to compete against each other.

But while racial segregation made it hard for Owens to compete as an athlete, it didn't stop him from becoming globally famous. While he retired from athletics not long after the 1936 Olympics, many people today still consider him to be one of the greatest short-distance runners of all time.

Owens was not invited to the White House after his incredible achievements at the 1936 Olympics. Although he finally received the invitation he deserved, in 1979, when President Jimmy Carter honored him with the Living Legend Award.

A career in sports was not an easy path for a young African American growing up in segregated America, but Owens never gave up.

The odds of Owens becoming a world-famous athlete were slim, which makes the fact that he managed to achieve this goal an inspiring reminder of what's possible.

JESSE OWENS HAD TO BEAT THE ODDS TO ACHIEVE SUCCESS AND REACH HIS FULL POTENTIAL

He proved that if you never give up, even when times are tough, you can achieve anything you set your mind to.

Over to You

We've met some truly inspiring people who overcame tremendous obstacles to achieve something great. They've faced different challenges and adversity, but they've never let that stop them.

Take Ernest Shackleton, for example. He and his men spent months camped out on the ice, waiting for a rescue ship that never came. Most people would have given up at that point. But he didn't. He fought for survival, and, against all odds, he and his men were able to make an epic journey back to safety.

Often, in those moments when things are tough, and you want to give up, you need to be the most courageous. It's in those moments that you have the opportunity to show your true strength and character.

It's unlikely that you'll find yourself stranded in Antarctica like Shackleton and his men were, but we all face challenges in our lives, both big and small.

How you DEAL WITH these CHALLENGES
DEFINES YOU AS A PERSON.

If you feel like giving up, remember the stories of the people above. Remember that they stuck it out, even when things were tough, and they were able to achieve great things because of this.

KEEP GOING. YOU CAN DO IT!

Activity - Things You Won't Ever Give Up

What is important to you? What are you passionate about?

What are some things you would never give up on, no matter how hard things got?

These things can be big or small. They can be anything that you feel really passionate about.

Think about the things that are important to you and write them down.

Then, for each thing, write down why you will never give up. What is it that keeps you going?

Here are some examples to get you started:

I will never give up on learning to play the piano, even though I've been taking lessons for years and still can't play very well. I enjoy the challenge and the satisfaction that comes with gradually getting better.

I will never give up on my dream of becoming a football player, even though I'm not the biggest or strongest guy on the team. I have a lot of heart and never give up, no matter the score.

I will never give up on my friends, even if they make mistakes or hurt me. I know that they're worth fighting for, and I'll always be there for them.

These things can be your guide in life, helping you to stay focused on what's truly important.

THINGS you WON'T ever give up...

I will never give up...

CHAPTER 4

TAKING RISKS & OVERCOMING FAILURE

I have NOT

FAILED.

I've just found

10,000 WAYS

that

WON'T WORK.

STARTUP

- Thomas Eddison

If you want to achieve something great, you need to be willing to take risks. You need to be ready to put yourself out there and fail. As we have already seen, failure is a part of success.

Now you might be thinking, "Why would I want to fail? That doesn't sound like a very good strategy."

But here's the thing:

IF YOU'RE NOT FAILING, YOU'RE NOT TRYING. AND IF YOU'RE NOT TRYING, YOU'RE NOT GOING TO ACHIEVE ANYTHING.

Let's put it another way.

Do you remember learning to ride your bike?

You probably fell off a few times, right? But you got back on and kept going. Eventually, you learned how to ride.

If you had given up after falling off the first time, you would never have learned how to ride. You would have just stayed where you were.

Because you were willing to take a risk and fail, you were able to achieve something great.

The same is true for anything in life.

SOMETIMES YOU HAVE TO FALL OFF YOUR BIKE BEFORE LEARNING HOW TO RIDE.

Each time you fall off, you learn something new — and without that learning, you won't move forward.

Don't be afraid to take risks and fail. It's part of the process. As the people in the stories below will show you, it's how you become successful.

Sir Richard Branson

ENTREPRENEUR (1950 – PRESENT)

Sir Richard Branson is a British billionaire who founded the Virgin Group. He is a successful entrepreneur, business magnate, and philanthropist.

You DON'T LEARN to WALK by FOLLOWING RULES. You LEARN by DOING, and by FALLING OVER.

– Richard Branson

Richard Branson knows a thing or two about taking risks. In fact, he's built his entire career on it.

From starting a record label to launching an airline, he has never been afraid to take calculated risks.

Richard Charles Nicholas Branson was born in London, England, on July 18, 1950. Growing up, he had dyslexia and struggled at school, performing poorly on tests. But that didn't stop him. In fact, he took his first step as an entrepreneur at age 11.

Branson and his friend saw a gap in the market to sell budgerigars (small birds) as pets, so they set about breeding them, only to have them multiply quicker than they could sell them. The business failed, as did the next one, where Branson grew Christmas trees, which were eaten by rabbits.

By age 16, Branson decided to drop out of school for good. Before he did, his headmaster told him that he would either end up in jail or become a millionaire. As it turns out, he was right on both counts!

Although Branson's first few businesses failed, he didn't give up. However, after leaving school and moving to London, reality set in. Times were tough. With no money and as a school dropout, he ended up living in the basement of a house owned by a friend's parents for a year.

While there, he had the inspiration to start a youth culture magazine called "Student," with the first issue hitting the streets in 1968. Inspired by the initial success of this venture, he started using the magazine to sell records by mail order when the magazine began to lose money.

 This side of the business eventually grew into a store in central London. In 1972, at age 22, Branson launched Virgin Records. This was a considerable risk. With minimal knowledge of the music industry, he was up against some of the biggest names in the business. But he had a vision, tenacity, and a willingness to work hard — and it paid off. The company went on to sign some of the world's biggest bands, including the Rolling Stones, Janet Jackson, and Simple Minds.

BRANSON WAS NOW A **MILLIONAIRE** AND ON HIS WAY TO CREATING THE VIRGIN GROUP, WHICH TODAY INCLUDES OVER **400 COMPANIES** IN MORE THAN **30 COUNTRIES**, EMPLOYING AROUND **50,000 PEOPLE.**

But perhaps his most considerable risk was starting Virgin Atlantic Airways, taking on the might of British Airways with just one second-hand Boeing 747 aircraft.

The idea came to him out of frustration. In the early 1980s, after his flight from Puerto Rico was canceled, he looked for a solution instead of sitting back and doing nothing. He hired a plane, borrowed a blackboard, and wrote "Virgin Airlines one-way: 39 dollars" as a joke. To his surprise, the flight filled up with all the canceled passengers — and Virgin Atlantic was born.

But it wasn't all smooth sailing. In 1992, Virgin Atlantic airline was close to bankruptcy after British Airways launched a dirty tricks campaign to put it out of business. Branson fought back and eventually won, turning Virgin Atlantic into one of the most successful airlines in the world, with over 5 million passengers a year.

Not all of Branson's businesses succeeded. Many failed, such as Virgin Cola, which tried to take on the might of Coca-Cola. It was a brave attempt but one that ultimately failed. But as always, Branson looked to the positive and saw this failure as motivation and a learning experience, ensuring he would not make the same mistakes again.

In addition to being a successful businessperson, Branson is a passionate adventurer and has often used his adventures to publicize his latest ventures. In 1987, he made headlines worldwide when he crossed the Atlantic Ocean in a hot air balloon. He followed this up a few years later when he was also in the first balloon to cross the Pacific Ocean.

In 2004, Branson set his sights on space with his latest venture, Virgin Galactic, working to make space travel possible for everyone. Hoping to have his first maiden spaceflight by 2010, he had to wait out setbacks and delays.

In July 2021, at age 71, Branson became the OLDEST PERSON to ENTER suborbital SPACE aboard Virgin Galactic's spacecraft "Unity."

In 1999, he was knighted by Queen Elizabeth II for "services to entrepreneurship," and for his charity work. In fact, he started his first charity, "Student Valley Centre," right at the start of his entrepreneurial journey when he was just 17 years old. He later established Virgin Unite, a non-profit foundation that he hopes will positively impact the world.

Richard Branson has led an extraordinary life. He has repeatedly taken risks and turned his many failures and struggles into the stepping-stones to success. His firm belief is that there is nothing wrong with making mistakes as long as you learn from them and don't make the same mistakes again.

Just like Branson, you can achieve anything you set your mind to.

TAKE CALCULATED RISKS AND INSTEAD OF FEARING FAILURE, LEARN FROM IT AND USE IT TO YOUR ADVANTAGE.

Above all, seize every opportunity that comes your way. Who knows what you might achieve!

William Kamkwamba

MALAWIAN INVENTOR (1987-PRESENT)

William Kamkwamba is an inventor, engineer, and author from Malawi who gained public recognition after building a wind turbine from collected scrap-yard parts to power his family's house.

> **☙ TRUST yourself and BELIEVE. WHATEVER happens, DON'T GIVE UP. ☙**
>
> **- William Kamkwamba**

Some of the greatest inventors in history were self-taught. William Kamkwamba is one of them.

Born on August 5, 1987, in Masitala Village in Malawi, Africa, Kamkwamba grew up in relative poverty on his family's farm with his parents and six sisters. At that time, many Malawian families like his relied on farming to survive, and less than 2% of rural Malawi had access to electricity. Instead, they relied on kerosene lamps and candles for light.

During the dry season of 2001, when Kamkwamba was 14 years old, drought hit Malawi hard. Crop yields were low, and food was scarce. Kamkwamba had to drop out of school because his parents could no longer afford the tuition, so he spent his days tending to the farm and looking for ways to help his family.

Even though he couldn't go to school anymore, Kamkwamba continued to educate himself by borrowing books from a small community library. There, he discovered an eighth-grade textbook called "Using Energy" with a photo of a wind turbine on its cover.

After reading "Using Energy," Kamkwamba decided to build his own windmill to generate electricity for his family's home. While most windmills often cost thousands of dollars to make and a college-level understanding of engineering, Kamkwamba constructed his from an assortment of reused parts found in the scrapyard.

AT JUST AGE 14, KAMKWAMBA TAUGHT HIMSELF TO BUILD A 16-FOOT WINDMILL MADE FROM A BROKEN BICYCLE, BLUE GUM TREES, A TRACTOR FAN BLADE, AND A SHOCK ABSORBER.

After hooking the windmill up to a car battery, it started working. His windmill was able to power his home and gave his family light at night.

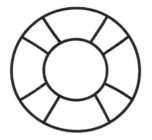 Soon his neighbors were also asking him to charge their appliances, too. Kamkwamba extended the windmill to 40 feet to catch more wind. He also added another windmill dedicated to pumping water.

Kamkwamba's homemade windmills drew much local attention and soon attracted journalists who reported on his success and innovative spirit. These articles later made their way to TEDGlobal Conference Director Emeka Okafor, who invited Kamkwamba to come to share his story at an event in Tanzania.

Kamkwamba's TED talk inspired several donors to fund his education and future projects. He continued his high school education at Lilongwe and attended the prestigious African Leadership Academy in 2008. A few years later, he earned his bachelor's degree in environmental studies from Dartmouth University.

After graduating, Kamkwamba worked with the WiderNet Project to help other Malawi students bring change to their communities. He also co-founded the Moving Windmills Project in 2008 to continue working with local leaders in

Malawi and develop new solutions to improve conditions on Malawian farms.

The story of Kamkwamba's homemade windmill has been celebrated around the world. In 2016, he released his memoir, "The Boy Who Harnessed the Wind: Creating Currents of Electricity and Hope," in which he recounts how he helped his community despite facing many obstacles. The book was later adapted into a movie.

Kamkwamba's journey shows us the importance of persistence and believing in yourself. Although he didn't have access to a traditional engineer's support, training, or materials, Kamkwamba invented his own path to his success and improved the lives of many people in his country.

From witnessing Kamkwamba's incredible feat, we can learn that each of us is capable of improving our communities in our own unique way. Like William Kamkwamba, we must see the problems around us and dream up new solutions.

Dwayne Johnson (The Rock)

WWE & ACTOR (1972-PRESENT)

Dwayne "The Rock" Johnson overcame failure to become one of the greatest wrestlers of all time and a Hollywood superstar.

Be HUMBLE.
Be HUNGRY.
And always be
the HARDEST WORKER
in the room.

- Dwayne Johnson

As a 17-year-old, Dwayne Johnson didn't seem destined for success. The teenager had earned a reputation for getting into fights and had been arrested "probably eight or nine times," by his own admission.

Fortunately, the actor and wrestler known as "The Rock" was passionate about American football. He credits this passion and the love he received from his parents for showing him a way forward that involved getting attention for the right reasons.

TODAY, JOHNSON IS ONE OF HOLLYWOOD'S
HIGHEST-PAID ACTORS.

The movies he has appeared in have generated an astonishing $10.5 billion worldwide. He's also considered one of the top professional wrestlers of all time. But to rise to these heights, Johnson had to work incredibly hard.

Born in California in May 1972, Johnson had a troubled childhood. He moved around a lot as a child, living in various places, such as Hawaii, New Zealand, California, North Carolina, Connecticut, Nashville, and Pennsylvania.

While his father, Rocky Johnson, was a legendary pro wrestler in the 1970s and 1980s, by the time Dwayne Johnson was 14, his family had very little money. They were evicted from their small apartment in Hawaii, and around the same time, his parents got divorced.

Johnson would never achieve his first goal of being a successful pro football player. While he received a full scholarship to play college football for the University of Miami, he didn't get  picked up by any NFL teams. And when he moved to Canada to turn pro, he was cut from the Calgary Stampeders lineup in 1995.

In 1996, he continued the family tradition by starting a career as a wrestler. His grandmother was one of the first female promoters in pro wrestling, and both his father and grandfather were professional wrestlers.

But Johnson endured a lot of hatred before he was embraced as a wrestler. During his first matches under the name Rocky Maivia, fans booed him and chanted insults.

Because of this, the WWE writers made Rocky "a heel," the name given to villains in wrestling with personas designed for the fans to hate.

The Rock was initially met with hostility but persevered, and his charisma quickly had the crowd cheering for him even though he was the bad guy.

He soon moved up the ranks in the over-the-top world of US pro wrestling. The king of colorful catchphrases was known for asking his audience, "Can you smell what The Rock is cooking?" He was also famous for calling his opponents "jabronis" and cutting them off in promo videos with the line, "It doesn't matter what you think!" In pro wrestling, the theatrics are more important than the sport itself, and The Rock's quick wit and skill on the microphone made him a fan favorite.

In 1998, The Rock won his first WWE championship; by 2000, he was a wrestling superstar. But at around the same time, he decided to take a risk and try his hand at professional acting, appearing as the Scorpion King in "The Mummy Returns" in 2001. Three years later, after breaking the record for the most WWE championship victories, he took another risk by making acting his full-time career.

Johnson's success as a full-time actor wasn't immediate. His big breakthrough occurred in 2011 when he appeared in his first film as part of the "Fast and Furious" franchise.

TWO YEARS LATER, HE WAS THE WORLD'S HIGHEST-GROSSING ACTOR.

Roles in other blockbusters, such as the "Jumanji" franchise, "San Andreas" and the Disney cartoon "Moana" (the latter of which saw him voice the role of demigod Maui) cemented his reputation as a Hollywood megastar.

Despite his colossal success, life hasn't been easy for Johnson. He has been open about his struggle with depression, which began with the failure of his football career. He has helped reduce the stigma attached to mental health challenges by talking about this publicly.

In 2006, Johnson starred in "Gridiron Gang," a film about prison inmates who start a football team. In an interview, he explained that his misspent youth prepared him for the role. "I know what it's like to fail. And frankly, I know what it's like to expect to fail too, especially at that age," he said.

FORTUNATELY FOR THE WORLD, BY TAKING RISKS AND WORKING HARD, DWAYNE "THE ROCK" JOHNSON WAS ABLE TO TURN HIS FAILURES INTO TRIUMPHS.

His story reminds us that there are no setbacks that can't be conquered on the journey toward fulfilling our potential.

Jack Ma

ENTREPRENEUR (1964 – PRESENT)

Despite enduring failure and rejection, Jack Ma persevered, founding the Chinese e-commerce site Alibaba and becoming a billionaire.

ONCE in your life, TRY SOMETHING. WORK HARD at something. TRY to CHANGE. NOTHING bad CAN HAPPEN.

- Jack Ma

In 2014, Jack Ma became the wealthiest man in China. The e-commerce site he founded, Alibaba, debuted on the New York Stock exchange with a market value of $231 billion, the highest initial public offering (IPO) of all time.

Alibaba, which Ma started with 18 friends in 1999, is now one of the world's largest corporations. But getting there was a long, arduous journey for Ma, a former English teacher born in Hangzhou, China, in 1964.

Ma's route to becoming a billionaire involved taking plenty of risks. For starters, in China during the mid-1990s, few people owned personal computers.

BUT MA WAS WILLING TO RISK EVERYTHING
FOR HIS BELIEF THAT THE INTERNET WAS THE FUTURE.

Ma only used the Internet for the first time on a trip to the US in 1995. He was so impressed by the World Wide Web's potential that he quit his job as a teacher and started one of China's first registered Internet companies that year.

In 1999, he founded Alibaba, a platform allowing businesses to sell to each other. He filmed the company's first meeting,

139

believing he was making history. "I think the Internet dream will not die," he told the Chinese media, who were still pretty skeptical about the future of the Internet at the time.

Another risk Ma took was starting a tech company without much technical knowledge. Unlike most tech billionaires, like Facebook's Mark Zuckerberg or Amazon's Jeff Bezos, Ma had no tech background. In fact, he has said that he doesn't really understand technology.

Rather than relying on his own knowledge, Ma has always let others lead the way in making the technology behind Alibaba  work, with his role being strategist, entrepreneur, and motivator for those around him.

Most people would only have the confidence to start an Internet-based company with technical knowledge of how this is done, but Ma is not most people. His success comes not only from his willingness to take risks but also from his personal philosophy of perseverance. He is a perfect example of someone who never gave up.

Ma's introduction to failure came early in life when he failed his primary school exams twice and his middle school exams three times. After high school, he applied to universities, failing the entrance exams three times before being accepted on his fourth attempt. He later tried to get into Harvard University 10 times and was rejected on each attempt.

Ma applied for a job at KFC when the fried chicken chain opened in China.

"24 PEOPLE WENT FOR THE JOB. 23 PEOPLE WERE ACCEPTED. I WAS THE ONLY GUY WHO WASN'T."

He was also the only person out of five applicants to be rejected when he tried to become a police officer.

While many people would have let such experiences get under their skin, Ma turned them into a positive. In fact, he felt his early failures helped him make Alibaba a success. In the early stages of the business, he heard the word "no" a lot, but his past failures allowed him to persevere rather than lose hope each time he faced another rejection.

 In 2010, Ma decided to donate a small percentage of the annual profits of his company to environmental causes, particularly those trying to make air and water cleaner. Never motivated by profits alone, he has said, "Our challenge is to help more

people to make healthy money, 'sustainable money,' money that is not only good for themselves, but also good for society."

Ma has also used his wealth to do good, making generous donations to environmental and social causes. This has included raising money for 10,000 houses destroyed by earthquakes in Nepal to be rebuilt, starting an organization to help young entrepreneurs, and opening a business school.

In 2018, he decided to leave Alibaba and start the Jack Ma Foundation, which focuses on education, the environment, and other vital causes.

Jack Ma is a true self-made man who persevered until he achieved great things and never let rejection stop him from striving for success.

HIS EXAMPLE SHOWS THAT ANYTHING IS POSSIBLE IF YOU TAKE RISKS AND OVERCOME THE FEAR OF FAILURE.

Over to You

In this chapter, we have met four inspirational people who have started businesses, built windmills to support their village, flown into space, and overcome obstacles to become a Hollywood superstar. Despite the differences in their achievements, they all took risks, which meant they faced the possibility of failure. In fact, they most likely experienced more failures along the way than anyone knows and probably still fail at things today.

That's precisely the point. Failure is built into their learning process. It's how they became successful.

As Michael Jordan, one of the greatest basketball players of all time once said:

"I'VE FAILED OVER AND OVER AND OVER AGAIN IN MY LIFE. AND THAT'S WHY I'VE BEEN SUCCESSFUL."

So instead of giving up or thinking, "This is too hard, I can't do it," ask yourself, "What's the worst that can happen if I try and fail?"

The answer is usually "not much." You might feel a bit embarrassed or disappointed, but you will survive. And in the process, you will learn something and be better prepared for next time — just like when you fell off your bike while learning to ride.

GET BACK UP, AND YOU TRY AGAIN.

Don't be afraid to take risks. You might surprise yourself with what you can achieve.

Activity - The Jar of Awesomeness

Sometimes, when things are tough, it can be hard to remember all the good things that have happened in your life.

The Jar of Awesomeness is where you can write down and store all your happy memories and achievements.

WHENEVER YOU'RE FEELING DOWN, YOU CAN TAKE OUT THE JAR AND READ THROUGH ALL THE GREAT THINGS THAT HAVE HAPPENED TO YOU.

To make your own Jar of Awesomeness, find a jar and decorate it however you like, then start filling it up with happy memories!

The Jar of AWESOMENESS

My Jar of Awesomeness

CHAPTER 5

DREAMING BIG & THINKING OUTSIDE THE BOX

SHOOT for the MOON. Even if you MISS, you'll LAND among the STARS.

- Norman Vincent Peale

Do you have a dream? Something you really want to do or achieve?

It could be something minor, like learning to play the guitar. Or maybe it is something bigger, like becoming a doctor or an astronaut.

Whatever it is, it all starts with a dream.

WHEN YOU DARE TO DREAM BIG,

AMAZING THINGS CAN HAPPEN.

Just ask the people in this chapter.

They all had big dreams and were willing to take risks and work hard to make them come true.

Louis Braille

EDUCATOR (1809 – 1852)

Louis Braille was a French educator who invented
the Braille reading and writing system for the visually impaired at 15.

BRAILLE is KNOWLEDGE, and KNOWLEDGE is POWER.

- Louis Braille

Sometimes it's easy to take the simplest things for granted, like being able to read and write. But for Louis Braille, this was only possible once he invented the Braille system.

Born on January 4, 1809, in the small town of Coupvray, France, he was the youngest of four children. His dad, Simon-René, was self-employed and worked as a saddler in the local village. Young Braille liked nothing better than to play in his dad's workshop with his tools and materials, but an accident with one of the tools changed his life forever.

As a three-year-old, Braille was attempting to make holes in a piece of leather with an awl (a pointed tool used for making holes). But the device slipped and punctured his right eye. In the weeks following the accident, infection set in, leaving Louis in agony. The infection then spread to his left eye. By the time he was five years old, he was blind.

Unusually for the time, Braille's parents wanted him to be raised as normally as possible and even obtain an education, despite being blind. When he was six, a priest gave him lessons for a year. But Braille wanted to be at school with other  children, so he enrolled in the local village school. He learned by listening and memorizing what the other children wrote down. Driven to succeed and not allowing his disability to affect him, Braille was one of the brightest boys in the school. Still, his parents were concerned about how their son would continue his education beyond what was available in their village.

When he was 10 years old, Braille and his dad set off for Paris to secure a spot for him at the Royal Institute for Blind Youth. It was the first school to offer education for blind students. Braille was accepted on a scholarship, but the conditions at the school were appalling. The building was dilapidated, dank, and damp, and the students weren't given much food. However, this did not deter Braille, and he quickly adapted to his new environment and made friends.

At the school, Braille now had the opportunity to read using a system of embossed raised alphabet letters. The letters were formed by pressing paper onto pieces of lead shaped like the letters of the alphabet. He also learned how to play the piano and cello by memorizing the notes. But despite being one of the brightest students, Braille could tell that many other visually impaired students struggled with deciphering the raised alphabet letters. This realization and a visit to the school by retired artillery officer Charles Barbier sparked Louis' inventive genius at just 11 years old.

Barbier had invented a code that used raised dots to represent different sounds so soldiers could communicate silently at night without alerting the enemy. The system did not succeed as a military tool, but Barbier thought it might be helpful for blind people. Chosen as one of the students to assess the system, Braille quickly recognized its superiority over the embossed alphabet reading system and set out to improve it.

In the following years, he worked during his free time at school and even during his summer vacation to perfect his system enabling blind people to read and write. In 1829, at age 20, Braille published the Braille code, a method that allowed the blind to read by moving their fingertips from left to right across a line of dots. Elated, he asked his classmates at school to try out his new code, and the results were remarkable.

Memorizing LONG class LECTURES was NO LONGER NECESSARY. Better yet, they didn't need anyone's help to read or write.

Braille wanted to give his gift to the world so other blind people could use it too. The school director, Alexandre François-René Pignier, was so impressed with the results of the system that he wrote to the French government to ask for the Braille code to be made the official writing system at the school. But the system was rejected and even banned by the new director, Pierre-Armand Dufau, who took over the school's administration shortly afterward. He was afraid there would be no need for sighted teachers at the school if everyone who was blind could read and write using the Braille system.

This did not deter Braille, who, although disappointed, continued writing books and music using his Braille system until ill health forced him to retire from teaching in 1850. Sadly, two years later, on January 6, 1852, Braille passed away at 43. But his legacy endures to this day. Two years after his death, the French government approved his system, which became known as Braille. And in 1878, the World Congress for the Blind voted to make Braille the official method of reading and writing worldwide.

Fast forward 170+ years, and Braille's code is still used as the universal system for touch reading for blind or visually impaired people today. Incredibly it has even been adapted for smartphones via refreshable Braille displays.

Despite his physical disability, Louis Braille proved that anything is possible with sheer determination and the right mindset. He followed his dream to open the doors of knowledge to all who could not see.

Remember, IT ALWAYS SEEMS IMPOSSIBLE UNTIL YOU DO IT.

No matter who you are, you can accomplish anything you set your mind to with the right attitude. Sometimes this means thinking outside the box to find solutions as you strive toward your dream. Just like Braille, you can do it too.

Stephen Hawking

PHYSICIST (1942 – 2018)

British academic Stephen Hawking was a world-re-
nowned physicist, cosmologist, and author who
overcame a diagnosis of motor neuron disease in
his 20s to make some of the most significant scientific discoveries of our time.

Remember to LOOK UP AT the STARS and NOT DOWN at your feet.

- Stephen Hawking

Born in January 1942, Stephen Hawking spent the first eight years of his life in Oxford, England, where he would later return to start his journey to brilliance at Oxford University.

While Hawking wasn't born into poverty, he didn't have it easy growing up. His grandfather was once a wealthy landowner but went bankrupt in the early 1900s. Hawking was raised during the Second World War, a financially devastating time for many families. His parents — a medical researcher and a secretary — struggled to support Hawking and his three siblings. However, the most significant challenges he would face were yet to come.

Just before Hawking turned 21 — not long after he earned his degree from Oxford — he was diagnosed with motor neuron disease (also known as Gehrig's disease). Motor neu- 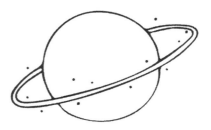 ron disease attacks nerve cells in the brain and spine, leaving those who suffer from it unable to control or move their muscles. He was told he had around two years left to live.

Hawking suffered from depression following the news of his condition. Still, he didn't let his deteriorating health stop his search to understand our universe. In fact, he decided to focus all his efforts on his studies and work because he believed that he wouldn't live much longer. In 1966, just three years after his diagnosis, he earned his Ph.D. in Physics at Cambridge University.

As Hawking's career progressed, his condition worsened. He was soon in a wheelchair and, by the late 1970s, could not move or speak. In 1986, with the help of new computer software, he was able to choose words that the software would vocalize, giving him a voice again.

Hawking's disability did not stop him from creating ground-breaking work. As he said, "Although I cannot move and I have to speak through a computer, in my mind I am free."

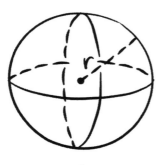

$$V = \frac{4}{3}\pi r^3$$

His research into topics such as black holes — a part of the universe where gravity is so strong that it is believed nothing, including light, can escape — led to many of his peers considering him one of the greatest scientific minds.

One of Hawking's most famous theories, named Hawking radiation, concluded that black holes can emit radiation. He later discovered that they can also emit particles or even explode into a fountain of sparks. These theories were initially controversial but have since been embraced as breakthroughs in quantum physics.

In 1986, Hawking released his book, "A Brief History of Time," which was intended for a non-scientific audience. It explained some of the most complex ideas in cosmology and physics, such as The Big Bang Theory, black holes, and the nature of time, in a way that is easy to understand. The book was an instant bestseller, with more than 25 million copies sold to date, and made him a household name.

Hawking continued performing research and publishing papers, some of which changed our scientific understanding of the universe. But while he was regarded as one of the most outstanding scientists of his generation, he was also known for his incredible sense of humor. He often appeared on popular TV shows, including "The Simpsons" and "Star Trek: The Next Generation."

In 2015, the film "The Theory of Everything" was released, telling the story of Hawking's life and work. The film was a huge success and won several awards.

Hawking passed away in 2018 at age 76, proving wrong the doctors who told him in his early 20s that he would only live for two more years. Despite all the physical barriers, he lived a full and active life, using the brilliance of his mind to change our understanding of the universe.

From the start of his career, Hawking dreamed big. His ultimate goal was to find a single theory that could explain the entire universe.

As he put it,

"I AM JUST A CHILD WHO HAS NEVER GROWN UP. I STILL KEEP ASKING THESE 'HOW' AND 'WHY' QUESTIONS. OCCASIONALLY, I FIND AN ANSWER."

Perhaps it was precisely this childlike quality — this sense of wonder and curiosity — that made Hawking an exceptional scientist.

The rare disease that Hawking suffered from did not define him. Instead, his inquisitive mind and thirst for knowledge are his lasting legacy.

Stephen Hawking shows us how big dreams and an ability to see things from new angles can allow human beings to unlock the mysteries of the universe.

Sammy Lee

ATHLETE (1920 – 2016)

Diver and doctor Sammy Lee was the first Asian American to win an Olympic gold medal for the US.

I was going to PROVE THAT, in AMERICA, I COULD DO anything.

- Sammy Lee

One day in 1932, a 12-year-old boy named Sammy Lee was driving through Los Angeles with his father. At the time, the city was hosting the Olympic Games, and Sammy asked his dad why the streets were so beautifully decorated.

His dad explained that it was for the Olympics, an event for "the best athletes in the world." The young boy vowed that he would one day be an Olympic champion.

To achieve this dream, Lee would have to overcome many obstacles. He was born in August 1920 to Korean parents, at a time when Asian people in the US were subject to many of the same segregation laws as African Americans.

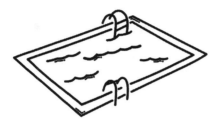

The local public pool where Lee learned to dive was reserved for white people, except once per week, on Wednesdays, the day before it was drained and refilled.

Amazingly, Lee turned the discrimination he suffered into an advantage. Because he could only use the pool once per week, he created his own place to practice — a diving board above a sandpit in his coach's yard.

WORKING WITH SAND RATHER THAN WATER MADE HIS LEG MUSCLES GROW VERY STRONG, GIVING HIM AN EDGE OVER OTHER DIVERS.

This is just one example of Lee's knack for turning negatives into positives. For instance, he was shorter than his peers, but this allowed him to tuck in tighter and turn faster than them while diving, transforming his small stature into an advantage.

Lee allowed the DISCRIMINATION
he suffered to motivate him rather than
DISCOURAGE HIM.

Born in the US, he considered himself American, not Korean and wanted other Americans to accept him as one of their own.

He eventually earned the respect of his fellow Americans on the diving board. He was soon well-known for his ability to execute perfect triple somersault dives.

 In 1942, he became the first Korean American to win the US Diving Championship. This began an athletic journey that saw Lee become the first Asian American to win an Olympic medal for the US and the first person to win gold medals at two Olympic Games in a row, in 1948 and 1952.

Lee wasn't just a diver — he was also a doctor. When his father said he thought that medicine was a safer path than athletics, Lee replied that he would do both. Adding a third career to his resumé, he also enlisted in the US Medical Corps, serving from 1947 to 1955.

Lee waited eight long years to prove himself at the Olympics, as the first two Olympic Games he had hoped to compete in, in 1940 and 1944, were canceled due to World War II.

War almost stopped him from competing in the Olympics again in 1952, as he felt a duty to serve in the Korean War. However, he was told by high-ranking officers to prioritize the Olympics. "Major Lee, we've only got one doctor who can win an Olympic gold medal. We've got hundreds of doctors who can repair the wounded. You can go, but you better win," a general told him.

After his military career, Lee practiced as an ear, nose, and throat doctor and visited 23 countries as a goodwill ambassador for the US. He also established the Sammy Lee Swim School in Orange County, California, offering swimming and, of course, diving lessons. He became a coach to young divers, some of whom went on to win their own Olympic medals.

He also helped in the fight against prejudice towards Asian Americans. When he returned home after his military service in 1955, he tried to buy a house in Orange County. He was turned down, and a real estate agent confided in him that he had been told not to sell homes to Asian people.

This story became a scandal in the American media, leading to an important legal decision in 1967. It was ruled that no state could allow private landlords to racially discriminate against potential buyers.

Lee was able to buy a home in Orange County, and a massive welcome party was thrown in his honor when his family moved in. "My belief in the American people is substantiated," he said at the event.

LEE'S SUCCESS BROKE DOWN BARRIERS, HELPING MAKE THE US MORE INCLUSIVE TOWARDS ASIAN AMERICANS AND OTHER GROUPS WHO SUFFERED DISCRIMINATION.

Sammy Lee became a national hero by dreaming big and thinking outside the box. His life demonstrates what human beings can achieve when they don't allow obstacles to stand in the way of success.

Albert Einstein

PHYSICIST (1879 – 1955)

Albert Einstein is one of the most famous scientists of all time. Born in Germany, he is best known for his theory of relativity. He was also a passionate humanitarian.

The true sign of INTELLIGENCE is not KNOWLEDGE but IMAGINATION.

- Albert Einstein

You might have heard of the word "genius" used to describe someone brilliant. The word actually comes from Latin, meaning "to produce." And that's what Einstein did — he produced some of the most groundbreaking scientific theories of all time.

But believe it or not, Einstein didn't do well in school when he was younger. In fact, it wasn't until he was older that he began to show his true potential.

Born on March 14, 1879, in the city of Ulm, Germany, Albert Einstein was the only son of a Jewish family. He did not talk until he was three years old, and even then, his parents thought he was "slow" because he took a long time to start speaking in whole sentences.

Many people considered Einstein a slow learner, but he was thinking about things differently. He daydreamed often and asked lots of questions, constantly asking his teachers questions they couldn't answer. Instead, Einstein preferred to learn by doing and experimenting on his own. By age 12, he had already taught himself geometry; by 15, he had mastered calculus.

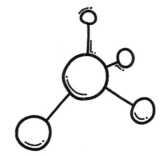

However, life got a lot tougher for young Einstein when his family moved to Milan, Italy, in June 1894, leaving him in Germany with relatives to complete his secondary education.

By December of that year, hating the strict discipline of the German school system, 15-year-old Einstein dropped out and joined his family in Italy. By then, he knew he wanted to pursue mathematics and physics and applied to the Zurich Polytechnic in Switzerland. But he failed the entrance exam. This did not deter Einstein. Instead, it inspired him to work even harder. In

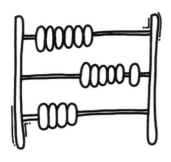

1896, he passed the entrance exam and qualified as a mathematics and physics teacher four years later.

Confident that he would get a job as a professor's assistant, he felt let down when none of his professors would accept him, as they thought he was arrogant. For the next two years, Einstein was mostly jobless until he finally found a position as a clerk in the Swiss patent office in Bern, Switzerland.

Einstein jumped at the chance, desperate for a job, but it was not the career he envisioned for himself. However, with plenty of time to think about physics, he continued to study in his spare time, and in 1905 he published four groundbreaking scientific papers, which included the famous equation $E=mc^2$. These four papers would change the world of physics and establish Einstein as one of the most outstanding scientists of all time.

In 1909, at age 30, he took up the first of many positions at prestigious institutions across Europe before settling at the University of Berlin, where he became a German citizen.

In 1919, Einstein's theory of relativity was proved correct when a British astronomer confirmed Einstein's prediction that massive objects cause a distortion in space-time. News of the theory's confirmation spread far and wide.

ALBERT EINSTEIN BECAME A HOUSEHOLD NAME AND WAS AWARDED THE NOBEL PRIZE IN PHYSICS IN 1921.

But it wasn't just his genius for physics that made Einstein a truly remarkable person. He was also a passionate humanitarian who realized that his fame made it possible for him to serve as a powerful advocate for the protection of human rights around the world. He believed that war could be prevented by cooperation among nations and that everyone should be treated equally. It was these views that brought Einstein to his next set of struggles in life.

Having traveled extensively, he considered himself a citizen of the world and spoke out about excessive nationalism. But during a visit to the United States in 1933, the storm clouds of war were building in Europe.

The Nazis, led by Adolf Hitler, had come to power and begun a campaign of persecuting the Jews. Many Jewish scientists lost their jobs and were forced to leave the country. As a Jewish scientist and a vocal activist against nationalism, Einstein was branded a "Jewish communist," which put him in imminent danger if he returned to Germany.

With no other option, Einstein was forced to renounce his German citizenship and flee to the United States. Although initially reluctant to move, he soon settled into his new life and became a professor at Princeton, New Jersey.

In the years that followed, Einstein continued to work on his theories. He continued to use his status to fight for the equal rights of African Americans. He was a tireless advocate for nuclear disarmament. The FBI even investigated him for 22 years, as the FBI director believed he was a spy.

Einstein died in the United States on April 18, 1955, at age 76, leaving behind a legacy that remains to this day. Despite his obstacles, he never backed down from his commitment to his work and principles.

HIS DETERMINATION TO SUCCEED SAW HIM LEARN FROM HIS FAILURES AND PURSUE HIS DREAMS TO THE VERY END.

In life, you will often encounter obstacles on your path to achieving your dreams. But it is how you navigate these obstacles that counts. Sometimes it takes more than determination and hard work to succeed. It takes self-belief and a willingness to never give up. Like Einstein, it's ok to make mistakes, but it's how you recover from them, move on, and use that experience to succeed that counts.

Over to You

To ACHIEVE GREAT THINGS IN LIFE, YOU HAVE TO DREAM BIG.

But everyone's dreams are different. Some people dream of becoming famous football players or actors, while others dream of becoming astronauts or politicians.

It is essential to find what you're passionate about and go after it with everything you've got.

Sammy Lee was passionate about diving. He didn't let anything stop him from achieving his dream of becoming an Olympic champion.

Louis Braille dreamed of inventing a system that would enable him and other visually impaired people to read and write. And he did precisely that at an astonishingly young age.

THE POINT IS THAT YOUR UNIQUENESS IS YOUR SUPERPOWER. IT'S WHAT MAKES YOU UNIQUE, AND IT'S WHAT WILL HELP YOU ACHIEVE YOUR DREAMS.

Activity - Think Outside the Box

As we have already seen, successful people approach problems creatively. They don't just accept things as they are but instead look for innovative solutions.

Like anything else, thinking outside the box is a skill that can be learned.

THE MORE YOU PRACTICE CREATIVITY, THE EASIER IT BECOMES.

Here's a fun activity to help you get started.

Instructions:

1. Take a look at the picture on the next page. It's incomplete.

2. Your task is to use your imagination to finish the picture. Think outside the box and be creative!

3. What did you come up with? What story does your picture tell?

THINK

OUTSIDE

the box

Complete the picture... it is NOT a dog...

Go get 'em!

If you CAN DREAM IT, you CAN ACHIEVE IT.

Whatever you want to be, wherever you want to go in life, don't let anyone stop you. Just keep going.

Things will be challenging; you'll have tough times and make mistakes. But if you don't give up and keep pushing forward, you will achieve anything you set your mind to.

So what are you waiting for? Go out there and make your dreams come true!

GO AND ACHIEVE SOMETHING GREAT.

All your DREAMS can COME TRUE, if you have the COURAGE to PURSUE them.

- Walt Disney

Now it's your turn... draw your portrait:

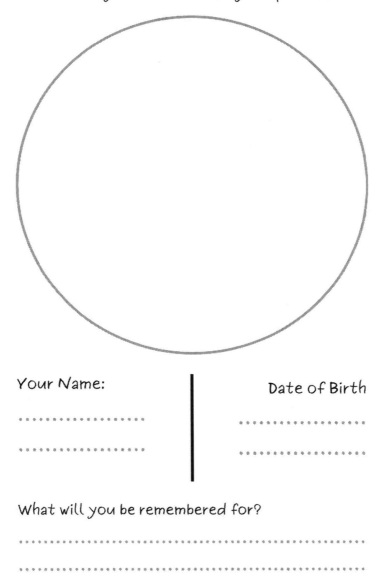

Your Name:

....

....

Date of Birth

....

....

What will you be remembered for?

....

....

What's your favorite quote? Write it down here:

Write your story:

FOLLOW
your DREAMS.
They KNOW
the WAY.

- Kobe Yamada

THANKS

FOR READING OUR

BOOK!

We sincerely hope you enjoyed it and that you and your child are motivated by the inspiring stories.

We would be so grateful if you could take a few seconds to leave an honest review or a star rating on Amazon. (A star rating takes just a couple of clicks).

Your review also helps other parents discover this book, and it might help their tween children on their journeys. Plus, it will also be good Karma for you.

To leave a review

SCAN HERE

LIKED THIS?
WE THINK YOU'LL
LOVE THIS!

"I wish I had this book when I was younger."

-Amazon Customer

Get your copy today.

SCAN HERE